YOU CAN MASTER MATH!

Let's Measure It

By Mike Askew

PowerKiDS press.

New York

Published in 2022 by The Rosen Publishing Group, Inc.
29 East 21st Street, New York, NY 10010

Editors: Ruth Owen and Mark J. Sachner
Designer: Emma Randall

Images courtesy of Ruby Tuesday Books and Shutterstock.

Cataloging-in-Publication Data

Names: Askew, Mike.
Title: Let's measure it / Mike Askew.
Description: New York : PowerKids Press, 2022. | Series: You can master math!
Identifiers: ISBN 9781725331631 (pbk.) | ISBN 9781725331655 (library bound) |
ISBN 9781725331648 (6 pack) | ISBN 9781725331662 (ebook)
Subjects: LCSH: Measurement--Juvenile literature.
Classification: LCC QA465.A85 2022 | DDC 530.8--dc23

Manufactured in the United States of America

CPSIA Compliance Information: Batch #CSPK22
For Further Informtion contact Rosen Publishing, New York, New York at 1-800-237-9932.

Contents

Measuring Me!

Get Ready

You will need:
- A ball of thin string or thick yarn
- Scissors
- A helper

Get your helper to measure your height with a piece of string.

Are You Square?

You can find out if you're square by doing some measuring with a helper.

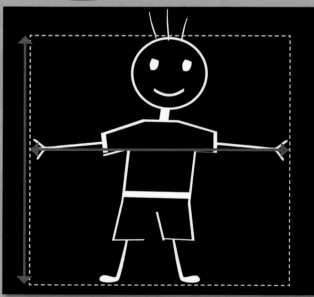

Next put your arms out wide. Your body span is the length from the tip of one hand to the other.

Get your helper to measure your body span with string.

If the piece of string for your height is the same length as the piece of string for your body span, you are square.

How square are you?

GO For It!

Measure your best friends or your family. Who is the most square?

4

Three Times Around Your Head

Get Ready

You will need:
- A ball of thin string or yarn
- Scissors
- A helper

Number 3 says:

Three times around your head is about the same as your height!

Let's check it out!

Ask your helper to wrap a length of string around your head three times.

They should make a mark on the string where it meets up with the start of the string.

Take the string off your head and cut it at the mark.

Compare the length of this string with the string that measured your height.

Was Number 3 right?

GO For It!

Compare other parts of your body. For example, how does the length from the tip of your middle finger to your elbow compare with the length of your foot?

Best Foot Forward

Try measuring the length of your bed with your feet.

Pigeon Steps

Start next to the end of your bed and measure its length in pigeon steps.

Put the heel of one foot so it touches the toes of the foot behind.

Keep pigeon-stepping and count how many steps.

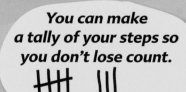

You can make a tally of your steps so you don't lose count.

Strides

Now measure the length of your bed in strides, or big steps.

Did it take more pigeon steps or strides to measure your bed? Why?

How many pigeon steps do you think it will take to cross the room? How about strides?

Write down your predictions and then check them.

GO For It!

Get an adult to measure your bed and room using pigeon steps and strides. Did they get the same numbers as you?

Biggest Smile

You will need:
- Paper and a pen or pencil
- Measuring tools, such as a ruler, tape measure, or string

Who has the biggest smile in your family?

How can you measure a smile?

You can use a piece of string.

You could hold a piece of paper to a person's mouth. Mark the corners of their smile on the paper and then measure from mark to mark with a tape measure.

You could take a close-up photo on a phone, print out the photo, and then measure the smile with a ruler.

Can you think of another way to measure a smile?

Now measure your family's smiles. Use the same method to measure each smile so you can compare your results.

Who has the biggest smile?

Measure people's mouths when they are not smiling.

Whose mouth widens up the most when they smile?

7

Make Marble Weights

You will need:
- 15 marbles or small stones
- 4 small sandwich bags
- Sticky tape
- Paper and a pen or pencil

1 ounce

2 ounce

4 ounce

8 ounce

People used to use weights called pounds and ounces.

Weights

Scales

Ounce weights were made to be used on scales.

You can make a set of weights using marbles.

1 Put one marble in a sandwich bag and seal the bag with sticky tape.

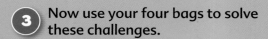

2 Make three other bags, one bag with 2 marbles, a bag with 4 marbles, and a bag with 8 marbles.

3 Now use your four bags to solve these challenges.

Can you use your bags of marble weights to make a weight of 7 marbles?

Can you make a total weight of 13 marbles?

Can you make all possible weights from 1 marble to 15 marbles by combining your bags?

Making Weight

Get Ready

You will need:
- Kitchen scales
- A 2-pound bag of flour
- Objects from around the kitchen

Put the bag of flour on the scales.

Look at the scales and notice what the scales are showing when something weighs 2 pounds (about 1 kg).

This mechanical scale shows metric units. It's showing 1 kilogram. That is about the same as 2 pounds.

WHOLE WHEAT FLOUR ORGANIC

WHOLE WHEAT FLOUR ORGANIC

32 oz

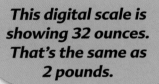

This digital scale is showing 32 ounces. That's the same as 2 pounds.

Can you find 10 different things in the kitchen that together weigh 2 pounds?

GO For It!

Can you find 20 different things that together weigh 2 pounds?

That's Handy!

You will need:
- Paper and a pen or pencil
- Yarn or string
- Scissors
- Some water

Round and Round Your Hand

Place your hand on the paper with your fingers closed and draw around your hand.

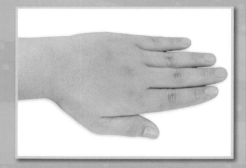 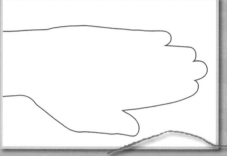 

How far would an ant crawl if it went all the way around the outside of your hand?

You can use the yarn to find out.

Carefully place the yarn around the hand outline on the paper. It will stay in place if you wet it with a little water.

Cut the yarn so you have a piece that's the same length as the distance around your hand.

How far would an ant crawl if it went all the way around the outside of your hand with your fingers spread apart?

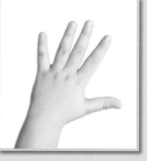 

Now draw around your hand with your fingers spread apart.

Measure the outline with another piece of yarn.

Which length is the longer?

Why do you think this is?

Four's Fantastic Facts

The distance around the outside of a shape is called the **perimeter**.

Get Ready

You will need:
- The outlines of your hand from page 10
- Lots of counters, buttons, or dried beans

Cover Up

Take the outline of your hand with the fingers closed.

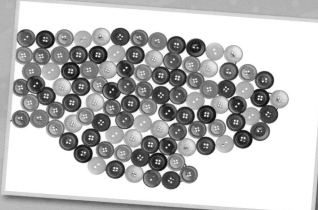

Carefully fill the hand shape with counters. Make sure they are placed close together.

Count how many you use and record your answer.

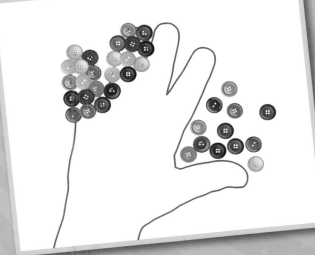

Now use counters to fill the outline of your hand with the fingers spread apart.

Count how many counters you use and record this answer.

How many counters did you use to fill each hand?

Why do you think you got the results you did?

Use yarn and counters to investigate the perimeter and area of your foot.

Four's Fantastic Facts

We call the space a shape covers the **area** of the shape.

Roll 'Em

You will need:
- Some big books
- A collection of objects that roll
- A tape measure
- Paper and a pen or pencil

To play "Roll 'Em" you will need plenty of space. A hallway is a good place to set up your investigation.

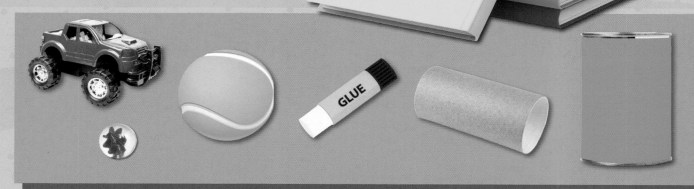

1 Make a ramp by leaning a book against a stack of other books.

2 Hold one of your objects at the top of the ramp. Let go and allow it to continue rolling until it stops.

3 Now examine each of your other objects.

Do you think each one will roll for a longer or a shorter distance than the first object?

Which object do you think will roll the farthest?

4 Record your predictions and then test them.

5 If you wish, measure how far from the bottom of the ramp each object rolls.

Make your ramp higher or lower by changing the number of books in the stack.

How does changing the height of the ramp affect how far things roll?

12

Leaf Prints

You will need:
- 2 leaves that are a different size and shape
- 2 sheets of paper that are the same size
- Paints and paintbrushes

Let's investigate "area" by making some leaf prints.

1. To print with a leaf, paint it with a thin coat of paint.

2. Press the painted side down onto the sheet of paper. You may be able to print two or three times before reapplying the paint.

3. Try to cover as much of the paper as possible with leaf prints. But do not let your leaf prints overlap.

   How many leaf prints did it take to cover the sheet of paper?

4. Now take the second sheet of paper and your second leaf.

   How many prints of this leaf do you think it will take to cover the paper?

GO For It!

5. Check your guess by printing with your leaf all over the paper. But remember, don't overlap the prints.

If you have finger paints, try covering a sheet of paper with handprints. Try it with your fingers closed. Then try it with your fingers spread open.

Timelines

You will need:
- Sheets of paper (one for every year of your age)
- Sticky tape
- Colored pens or pencils
- Photos of you and your family

My Story

Make a timeline of your life.

1 Label a sheet of paper with the year you were born. Label the next sheet with the year after that. Keep going until you reach this year.

2 On the paper for this year, draw a picture of yourself now or stick on a photo.

3 Now work backwards, drawing pictures or sticking photos for things that have happened to you in each year.

4 Finally, stick your sheets of paper together to make one long strip.

2014

The year you were born

2015

Moving to a new house

2016

A new brother or sister

2017

A new pet

2018

First day at school

2019

A birthday party

2020

Going on a plane for the first time

2021

You today

5 Use your timeline to tell the story of your life to your family, friends, or teacher.

You will need:
- 12 sheets of paper
- Sticky tape
- Pencils, pens, or paints

Take your first sheet of paper and label it "January." Then label the second sheet "February."

1 Keep going and write each month of the year on a separate sheet of paper.

2 Now join your sheets of paper together to make one long strip.

3 Draw or paint something that you do in each month and make a timeline of your year.

What kinds of things do you do in each month of the year?

January   February   March   April   May   June

July   August

September   October

November

December

You might build a snowman in January.

Perhaps you visit Grandma for her birthday in June or go on vacation in August.

In October, it's time to dress up for Halloween!

Fill a Box

You will need:
- A small box (such as a ring box, matchbox, or raisins box)

You can only have one of each type of thing in the box.

How many things can you fit into your box?

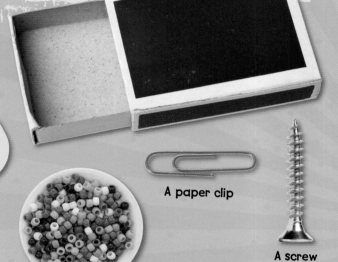

Here are some ideas to get you started!

A paper clip

A single rice grain

A bead

A screw

A flower petal

A cornflake

A button

A grain of salt

When your box is full, count how many different items it was able to hold.

Four's Fantastic Facts

We call how much a box or other container can hold its **capacity**.

GO For It!

Make this a family competition. Everyone has the same size box and a week to fill it. The winner is the person with the highest number of different things in their box!

Order & Check

Get Ready

You will need:
- A collection of 6 food objects from the kitchen, such as boxes, packets, or jars
- Paper and a pen or pencil
- Kitchen scales

Can you put things in order by how much they weigh? Let's go for it and find out!

1 Gather together six things from the kitchen cupboards. Look for things that are different sizes and weights.

2 Pick up two of your objects and hold one in each hand.

Which feels heavier?

Now swap hands.

Does the same object still feel heavier?

3 Keep comparing pairs of objects until you think you have found the heaviest one. Put that object to one side. Write or draw what it is on your sheet of paper.

Now use the kitchen scales to check if you got the order right.

4 Now decide which object you think is the next heaviest. Put it beside the first object. Record what it is.

5 Keep going until you have all the objects in order, from what you think is the heaviest to the lightest.

Pour & Check

Begin by collecting six containers from around your kitchen.

Get Ready

You will need:
- A collection of 6 containers from the kitchen
- Paper and a pen or pencil
- Water
- An empty yogurt cup

Look for containers that are different shapes and will hold different amounts of water.

Saucepan

Cup

Empty glass jar

Vase

Plastic box

Jug

1 Take two of your containers. Look at them carefully.

If you pour water into each container, which do you think will hold more water?

2 Keep looking and comparing pairs of containers until you think you have found the one that will hold the most water.

I think the jug will hold the most water!

3 Put that container to one side. Write or draw what it is on your paper.

4 Now decide which container you think is the next size down. Put it beside the first object. Record what it is.

Keep going until you have all the containers in order, from the one you think will hold the most water to the one you think will hold the least water.

Container 1   Container 2   Container 3   Container 4   Container 5   Container 6

Now check if you got the order right!

5 Fill Container 1 with water.

Then pour water from Container 1 to fill your yogurt cup.

Make a tally to show you have filled the yogurt cup once.

> Container 1
> Jug
> ─────────
> |

6 Empty the yogurt cup. Fill it again from Container 1. Make another tally.

Keep pouring and making tallies until Container 1 is empty.

How many yogurt cups of water did Container 1 hold?

> Container 1
> Jug
> ─────────
> |||| |||| ||||
> |||| ||

7 Now use the yogurt cup to find out how much water each of the other containers will hold.

8 When you've tested all six containers, look at your tallies.

Did you have the containers in the right order?

19

Make a Measuring Jug

Get Ready

You will need:
- An empty plastic bottle (one with smooth sides is best)
- Scissors
- An adult helper
- Sheet of paper
- Sticky tape
- An empty yogurt cup
- A black marker

Get ready to do some measuring using your own homemade measuring jug!

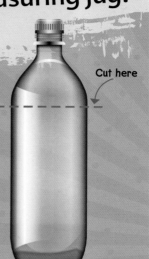

Cut here

1 Ask an adult to cut off the top part of the bottle.

Keep both parts of the bottle. You don't need the cap.

2 Cut a strip of paper and tape it to the side of the bottle.

3 If you wish, you can turn the top part of the bottle upside-down and sit it in the bottom part to create a funnel.

4 Now fill the yogurt cup with water. Pour the water into the bottle.

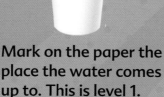

Mark on the paper the place the water comes up to. This is level 1.

1

2

1

5 Fill the yogurt cup again and pour it into the bottle. Mark this as level 2.

20

6 Keep refilling the yogurt cup and pouring water into the bottle. Mark the level each time.

When the bottle is full pour away the water.

Four's Fantastic Facts

You have made your own measuring jug, or **measuring cylinder**. The numbers on the side of the cylinder are called a **scale**.

Now you can use your measuring cylinder to do some measuring.

Find 3 containers:

How many yogurt cups of water does each container hold?

In turn, fill each container with water. Then pour the water into your measuring cylinder. Look at the scale and read off the measurement.

My Wacky Day

What things do you do every day? What would happen if you had a mixed-up, wacky day?

1 Take your sheet of paper and fold it in half. Then fold it in half again. And finally fold it in half one more time.

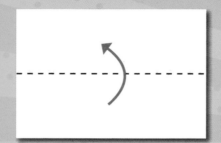

Next, unfold your paper and you should have made 8 sections.

2 Number the sections from 1 to 8.

1	2	3	4
5	6	7	8

At what time do you do these things?

3 Now think about the things you do from getting up in the morning to going to bed at night.

For example:
- You get out of bed.
- You get dressed.
- You get washed.
- You eat breakfast.

4 Choose 8 things that you do in a day.

5 Draw a picture for each thing you have chosen. Draw one thing in each box on your paper. You can also draw a clock that shows the time.

6 Cut up your paper into 8 separate pieces.

Here are some ideas for the kinds of things you could draw.

1

I wake up.

2

I eat breakfast.

3

I walk to school.

4

I eat my lunch.

5

I go swimming.

6

I eat my dinner.

7
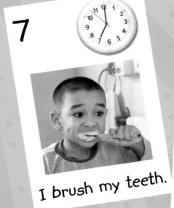
I brush my teeth.

8

I go to bed.

GO FOR IT!

Now it's time to play Wacky Day.

Put the pieces of paper face down on the table and mix them up.

Turn over the pieces of paper one at a time and tell the story of your wacky day.

For example:
I woke up.
Then I ate my dinner.
Then I walked to school.
Then I ate my breakfast!

Just a Minute!

What can you do in a minute?

You will need:
- Paper and a pen or pencil
- A cell phone with a timer

You could try drawing lots of stars.

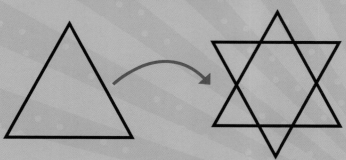

You can make a star by drawing a triangle. Then draw another upside-down triangle on top.

Get ready for your challenge by practicing drawing stars.

Now set the timer on the phone for one minute and GO FOR IT!

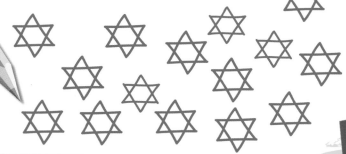

STOPWATCH

45

START   STOP

How many stars did you draw?

Try again! Did you manage to draw more stars the second time?

Four's Fantastic Facts

There are 60 seconds in 1 minute.
There are 60 minutes in 1 hour.

GO For It !

Test your family and friends. Who is the fastest one-minute-star-drawer?

How many times can you write your name in one minute?

How high can you count in one minute?

24

Calendar Patterns

On your calendar, draw a square around four dates.

You will need:
- A calendar page showing a full month (it can be an old one)
- A pen or pencil

Add the date in the top left-hand corner of your square to the date in the bottom right-hand corner.

11 + 19 = 30

Now add the date in the top right-hand corner of your square to the date in the bottom left-hand corner.

12 + 18 = ?

What do you notice?

Try drawing another square around four different dates.

Does the same thing happen?

MAY 2021

SUN	MON	TUE	WED	THU	FRI	SAT
						1
2	3	4	5	6	7	8
9	10	11	12	13	14	15
16	17	18	19	20	21	
23	24	25	26	27	2	29
30	31					

Go For It!

What happens if you add the opposite corners on a three-by-three square?

MAY 2021

SUN	MON	TUE	WED	THU	FRI	SAT
						1
2	3	4	5	6	7	8
9	10	11	12	13	14	15
16	17	18	19	20	21	22
23	24	25	26	27	28	29
30	31					

Victoria's Sponge

Get Ready

You will need:
- 4 eggs
- Soft butter
- Superfine sugar
- Self-rising flour
- A teaspoon of vanilla extract
- Kitchen scales
- A mixing bowl
- A wooden spoon
- A little butter for greasing
- 2 6-inch cake tins
- Oven gloves
- Raspberry jam and a spoon
- An adult helper

Look at Grandmother Victoria's sponge cake recipe. How does she know what quantity of each of the ingredients are needed?

Victoria's Sponge Recipe
4 eggs
butter
superfine sugar
flour

Grandmother Victoria knows a special measuring trick!

1 First weigh the eggs. Your scale might show grams, ounces, or both. These eggs weigh 270 grams. That's about 9.5 ounces.

2 Now measure out the same weight of butter as the weight of the eggs.

3 Next, measure out the same weight again of sugar and flour.

Great measuring! You're all set to get baking.

How to Make Victoria's Sponge

1 Ask an adult to help you switch the oven to 340°F (170°C).

2 Grease the cake tins with a little butter to keep your sponge cake from sticking.

3 Put the butter and sugar into the mixing bowl. Beat the ingredients with a wooden spoon until the mixture is light and fluffy.

4 Add the eggs one at a time, beating them into the mixture.

5 If you wish, you can add a teaspoon of vanilla extract. Stir it in.

6 Add the flour to the mixture and gently stir it into the other ingredients.

7 Divide the mixture equally between the two cake tins.

8 Ask an adult to help you put the cakes into the oven. Bake them for about 25 minutes.

GO For It!

When your cakes have cooled, you can sandwich them together with jam. Put a teaspoon of jam on the bottom cake and spread it. How many spoons of jam do you estimate it will take to cover the sponge cake with a thick jammy layer?

Ruler Race

Before you begin playing, each player draws a chart to record their Ruler Race measurements.

	Ruby		
Dice Total	Object	Measurement	Score

1 Player One (Ruby) throws the three dice and adds up the score:

$$5 + 5 + 3 = 13$$

2 Player One records their dice total on their chart. Then they throw the dice four more times, recording the total each time.

	Ruby		
Dice Total	Object	Measurement	Score
13			
3			
8			
18			
5			

3 Next, Player Two (Sam) throws the dice five times and records their totals.

4 Now, the players have 5 minutes to find 5 items that are the length of their dice scores. Pick whether to play in inches or centimeters.

The players cannot measure the items during their search, but must estimate if the objects are the correct length.

Ruby and Sam chose to play in centimeters (cm). Ruby must find items that are 13 cm, 3 cm, 8 cm, 18 cm, and 5 cm long.

5 The timer is set, and the race begins!

6 When the time is up, the players use their rulers to measure the objects they've found.

GLUE

← 7 cm →

← 3 cm →

← 11 cm →

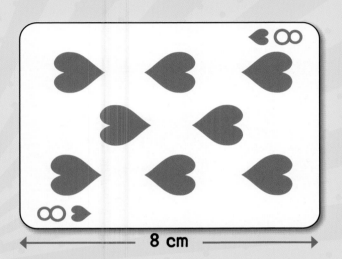

← 8 cm →

↕ 10 cm

If an object is the exact measurement or within 1 cm (if playing in inches, 1/2 inch) of the dice score in either direction, that's a point. If there is more than this difference, no point is scored.

	Ruby		
Dice Total	Object	Measurement	Score
13	Book	16 cm	✗
3	Coin	3 cm	✔
8	Playing card	8 cm	✔
18	Pencil	11 cm	✗
5	Glue stick	7 cm	✗

	Sam		
Dice Total	Object	Measurement	Score
18	Book	19 cm	✔
3	Lego	3 cm	✔
10	Teddy	10 cm	✔
12	Glasses	13 cm	✔
7	Purse	11 cm	✗

Sam is the winner of this game with 4 points!

GO For It!

You can also try playing Ruler Race with four dice or just two dice.

Tips for Math Success

Pages 4—5: Measuring Me!

Measuring is all about comparing. In "Are You Square?" learners get to compare their height with their body span without needing to use any units. You and your child might enjoy looking up da Vinci's Vitruvian Man online — perfectly square!

Page 6: Best Foot Forward

A core idea for learners to understand in measuring is that the larger the unit, the fewer of them will be needed. This activity explores this inverse relationship in two different ways: by comparing pigeon steps with strides and learners' measurements with yours.

Page 7: Biggest Smile

Measuring things in real life is often more difficult than measuring on the page of a book. This is a light-hearted activity to encourage learners (and you) to find some inventive ways of measuring something that's not usually or easily measured.

Page 8: Make Marble Weights

If you have a set of balance scales, learners can use this to put their bags of marbles on one side and weigh out quantities of rice or dried pasta on the other. Ask around to find out if anyone you know has an old set of ounce weights for learners to investigate.

Page 9: Making Weight

Having a sense of what certain weights feel like provides a good benchmark for estimating weights. Follow up this activity when you go shopping — does a cabbage weigh more or less than two pounds? What about a bag of onions?

Pages 10—11: That's Handy!

Learners often get confused about the difference between area (the amount of flat surface something covers) and perimeter (the length around the outside of an area). These activities provide the opportunity to introduce these ideas in a fun and informal way. Learners should discover that the perimeter of their hand is longer when their fingers are splayed out, but the area stays about the same.

Page 12: Roll 'Em

Learners can also try investigating the distance an object travels from different starting points on the ramp. They could also try attaching some cargo (such as modeling clay) to a toy car to see how this affects the distance it rolls. Talk to them about "fair tests." For example, make sure that the objects start at the same place on the ramp when they are being compared.

Page 13: Leaf Prints

Area is a measure that learners usually master later than length or weight. Print-making activities are a good way to help them get a sense of covering a surface with a repeated unit — a key part of understanding area.

Pages 14–15: Timelines

Making a timeline of their personal life history or of the things they do over the course of a year will help learners start to think about time. It will also help them to understand how to put events into chronological order. Making timelines is also a great way to help them recognize and use language relating to dates, months, and years.

Page 16: Fill a Box

Capacity is a difficult measure. This challenge provides a way of talking about the capacity of a box. It also helps learners understand the idea that even something as small as a matchbox can sound as though it is very large if the things being used to measure it are very small.

Page 17: Order & Check

Length is the easiest measure because we can often see which is longer. We do not need a ruler to decide if we are taller or shorter than someone. But impressions can be deceiving when it comes to weight. A small box or other container may be heavier than a large one. Putting items from around the kitchen in order of weight will help learners' understanding of what measured properties are all about.

Pages 18–19: Pour & Check

Again, impressions can be deceiving when it comes to capacity. For example, a tall thin vase may hold less water than a short wide bowl. Putting items from around the kitchen in order of how much water they hold will help develop learners' understanding of capacity and volume.

Pages 20–21: Make a Measuring Jug

Creating a measuring scale in this way will help learners understand how measuring involves repeatedly using the same unit. Challenge them to use their device to measure out set quantities — for example, 3 yogurt cups of water or 4 yogurt cups of uncooked rice.

Pages 22—23: My Wacky Day

Talking about and putting in order pictures of everyday activities provides learners with the opportunity to develop the language associated with time and the order in which things happen. If learners are not yet telling the time, simply draw the different activities without adding clocks but use time-related words such as morning, afternoon, and evening.

Page 24: Just a Minute!

Help learners get a sense of the duration of a minute by challenging them to get better at a simple task. Encourage them to be creative and to think about other one-minute challenges they could try.

Page 25: Calendar Patterns

Calendars are a rich source of number patterns. The answer to the two sums should be the same. By checking if this always works, learners will get plenty of addition practice.

Pages 26—27: Victoria's Sponge

This activity works well if you have access to some old-fashioned balance scales. Put the eggs on one side and measure out the other ingredients on the other side. If you have digital scales or scales with a circular dial, weigh the eggs, get learners to write down the result, and use this measurement to weigh out equal amounts of the butter, sugar, and flour.

Pages 28—29: Ruler Race

This fun game gives learners plenty of practice at adding, estimating lengths, and measuring with a ruler. It will also help give them a sense of how long a time period, such as five minutes, will last. Players will find that an object such as a playing card or book has sides of different lengths. Therefore, it might not be helpful for the measurement they originally intended, but could be useful for one of the other numbers they are trying to find. The more they play, the better their estimating skills will become. If they enjoy playing Ruler Race, it can be made more challenging with a shorter time allowed for the search or different numbers of dice to potentially give bigger or much smaller measurements to find.